THE PASTORACLASM

T0347014

RECENT POETRY COLLECTIONS INCLUDE

Shades of the Sublime and Beautiful (Picador, 2008)
Armour (Picador, 2011)
Sack (Picador, 2014)
Drowning in Wheat: Selected Poems (Picador, 2016)
Speak from Here to There with Kwame Dawes (Peepal Tree Press, 2016)
The Wound (Arc Publications, 2018)
A New Beginning with Kwame Dawes (Peepal Tree Press, 2018)
Insomnia (Picador, 2019)
Tangling with the Epic with Kwame Dawes (Peepal Tree Press, 2019)
Brimstone: A Book of Villanelles (Arc Publications, 2020)
In the Name of our Families with Kwames Dawes (Peepal Tree Press, 2020)
UnHistory with Kwame Dawes (Peepal Tree Press, 2022)

John Kinsella
The Pastoraclasm

SALT

CROMER

PUBLISHED BY SALT PUBLISHING 2023

2 4 6 8 10 9 7 5 3 1

Copyright © John Kinsella 2023

Ken Evans has asserted his right under the Copyright, Designs and
Patents Act 1988 to be identified as the author of this work.

*This book is sold subject to the condition that it shall not, by way of
trade or otherwise, be lent, resold, hired out, or otherwise circulated
without the publisher's prior consent in any form of binding or cover
other than that in which it is published and without a similar condition
including this condition being imposed on the subsequent publisher.*

First published in Great Britain in 2023 by
Salt Publishing Ltd
12 Norwich Road, Cromer, Norfolk NR27 0AX United Kingdom

www.saltpublishing.com

Salt Publishing Limited Reg. No. 5293401

A CIP catalogue record for this book is available from the British Library

ISBN 978 1 78463 284 7 (Paperback edition)

Typeset in Sabon by Salt Publishing

Printed and bound in Great Britain by Clays Ltd, Elcograf S.p.A

to the biosphere

Contents

Hymn of the Garden: a prologue

Always the hope of abundance,
    a garden is complex –
what grows where and how –
    the results will show.
Silvereyes and thornbills
    eat their fill,
a sun skink basks on the edge
    of a raised bed.
Some plants are insect repellents,
    some work as masking agents –
the lush growth you seek to protect
    against certain insects
while other insects you celebrate
    as they pollinate.
The contradictions of the garden,
    the syntax of contradictions.
Always the hope of abundance,
    to distract from presence.
What grows where and how –
    what in drought can glow?
Always the hope of abundance,
    a garden is complex.

Qualifying Ode to Experience

'The world is all that is the case.'
WITTGENSTEIN

but not a newsfeed, not really . . .

A person isn't a noun or an abstract noun.

When the termites swarm over dry tracts
after sudden wet, after deluge, after the rise
of moisture mocks the dryness and threatens
caltrop as the only viable greenery, they –
winged termites – reconfigure locality,
at least for the sake of their wings,
such casual attachments to limbs,
quick to shed as pheromones
are dished out – flight is not
as wonderful in itself, these crappy
flappers who will chance upon the best
outcome, from ground from nest to lovely
rotten wood surface ripe for mastication
and digestion and a new colony. It's
not wonderful being inside the bad joke,
but the act of experiencing and telling
is – in the circumstances – a display
of the joke being on one's self.

A termite isn't a noun or an abstract noun.

What's left after the swarmers
have expended their moment, when
heat has set in to sap the dry, is the event
of black house ants removing wings

and the deceased from window frames.
It would be carnage but it's really
a 'clean-up', and we over-invest
our role, having a householder's say.
Irony is the radar showing a storm
where there is none and failing to warn
when one comes down like endgame.
A poor workman blames the tools?
This technology of experience, of setting
out to sets roots anew, a conflict of tenses.

But wow, seriously, things are burgeoning –
where out of the months of dry, out of ashen air,
has all this life come? Praying mantises,
dwarf skinks, gerygones, all ecstatic and meticulous
in the frenzy of flying termites: the coming
out that is cataclysm and wonder, and I've
nothing meaningful to add other then, Hey,
we too are overwhelmed by water – drinking,
washing, soul-soothing water. Even erosion
can be a terraforming in the novelty,
and old scripts recycled to make new sense.

A bird isn't a noun or an abstract noun.

A heavy rustling outside – I expect
a monitor but it is a heavily pregnant
bobtail swaying side to side as it sweeps past,
that deft and heavy-slow quickness, that extra-
curricular to come but fine-tuned knowledge

[3]

to other observers – immersion, frequency,
everyday familiarity. Knowledge systems
at variance, in sync when necessary
for those on the ground? Semantics
can mess up the description but not
the allegiances, the vast memory
of experience: ticks under scales,
in ears, clustered, and yet the moisture
is stirring the shaping of organs, fast. Consciousness
is the vast release of energy consuming galaxies.

A person isn't a noun or an abstract noun
and nor is an animal or plant, or the earth,
so that leaves objects made to be admired,
and we are none of these. It's an echo of the crux
of a praying mantis's front legs, the mimicry
of its capturing. Such blanks in ontology
are links in the conveyer belt, the rare earths
of storage that lies about time, about species.

What motifs grab the crags of speech, settle
in the softest places of the mouth, flicked
by the tongue? Turn the sound down on one
of the three television stations you can still
receive – there is no intention to update
technology – and in the lip-synch dropout,
in the delay between shout and sound,
the grark! then sound off and picture
staggering along, to listen to the grark
graark . . . rrrrrrrrr . . . rrrrr . . . grark . . . grark . . .

of the owlet nightjar, super-audible despite
the terrifyingly high easterlies that mock
all the labour and exploitation and hype
that went into making that movie . . . nightjar
perusing same locale as usual – by the great
tank now recharged up to the algal-leak eye,
the visionary crack that brings spiritual
clarity in its pragmatic outcomes: daybirds
often gather to drink in the eminence of heat
of concrete walls, the friable air, but do nightjars
venture there in the way we hear them make
contact with windows and flyscreens, picking
off swarmers and solitary insects drawn
to the artificial light? Recurrence is not motif,
but maybe I compensate for the lake of channels,
the flawed vision, the disrupted soundtracks?
No, it's always been like this: it's my birdbrain
reaching out to voice other perspectives,
but those little to do with flight or feeding.

An owlet nightjar isn't a noun or an abstract noun.

To whom and why in the spread so many deny,
the address to a fallen tree they fell indirectly,
to the house settling where the swamp was
excavated? Each degree, each distraction –
the sun overwhelms and holds our senses
as source and aim of our apostrophes,
arrangement of song we are swept
away by. It's glib in the recording studio

if the noise of commerce can't be accounted
for, cancelled out. These textures of visible song,
mostly felt through the skin, but also as idea
of bird and word, the having been there, experienced.
All lucked out, something like 'atrabilious'
and the egg-kick of the cuckoo can add up
into a compulsion to augment our murmurs.

A person isn't a noun or an abstract noun.

Please don't think this any less hallowed
or holy for the secular nest, for the lack
of role-players in costumes leant by restraints –
here there are doses of belief that don't fit
and run against sap, making claims
that ruffle the feathers of birds losing
their mates, or corella flocks brought down
from the skies, scattered bloody over paddocks.

A corella isn't a noun or an abstract noun.

I can't give you anything and I can't take
anything from you, objective corellative: cloudy,
it burns harder and deeper and the search
for a cure gains pace: out of love of one another,
and for profit. The rub, just as thunder and lightning
are made, tilts entire agglomerations of people
towards a solitary figure in a field, on a mountain,
staring into a chasm. Volcanoes ring the edges,
fiery even in extinction. From a land of conflagration.

You don't get to write about termite galleries
once and move on, unless you've saturated
the world in toxins so deadly they measure presence
in decades centuries maybe in a sense forever.
So I get outside and clear along the front
of the house between path and slab – raking
away the leaf litter, letting mimetic grasshoppers
and praying mantises move away at their own
pace – quick hop, then hop back . . . scissor leg
angle-poise lamp postures to take me on, and I retreat
from the mantis, whose eyes consume me. Motifs,
refrains and that strong bloody wind agitating
dust and sand as I scrape away to keep the slab
above ground clear from a heavy swell, from tubes
for termite surfers to house consciousness,
to plan their galleries, to climb higher into walls
and the wood of books, the grotesque intrusion
of the written word, the picture plates, the facsimiles
of languages from the Mediterranean, ruins from
ancient Ireland, Sanskrit, Persian from Persepolis,
poems in exquisite calligraphy from the T'ang
Dynasty – all in this house perched on the side of a valley
where the eroded has been eroded further down
to consequence, to words of bodies and rocks,
where termites build across the divides making truth,
recycling, translating, transcribing, undoing, restating.
And also say, over, Mimetic gumleaf grasshopper,
mimetic gumleaf grasshopper mimetic gumleaf.

A praying mantis isn't a noun or an abstract noun.

And then the sound of preta-conflagration
the sound of deathgrind the rain of sparks
the reign of terror the grinder on a summer's
afternoon the wind to carry the embers of oblivion.

A person isn't a noun or an abstract noun.

In the breath of the world is the breath-destroyer
that should never have been – locked away in tissue,
prodded in labs, the level 4s that dot the planet
as distillations of hubris. There are many
manifestations of stockpiles and isolation,
but trade and travel won't let anyone go:
humans traversing in machines is mass
death for animals. Birds chewed up in the sky.
The choke-hold of smoke, of pollutants,
the failure of respiration as well treats
the sky-lungs as membranes we can pass
through and through and though. Impunity.
The unpleasant interruption to an idyll.

An animal isn't a noun or an abstract noun.

Wings everywhere – wings looking for their
matching partner, to pair, to make possibility
for renewal, redemption. To be taken on to lift
again, brown filaments, curved ends of a fan,
animal tissue leaves that flitter around if a page
is turned, a creature passes, stirring. Wings
everywhere, after the fact, gradually carted

away by ants of all sizes, taken back under-
ground in different circumstances, different
kinds of tunnels, different chambers – but still,
that earthy smell, that air so close and absent,
that spiracle to trachea that bloodless journey
of oxygen molecules under, under, and wings
of ants will form for nuptial days as well –
different wings, their wings, falling everywhere
from their bodies, their bodies made in part
at least from termite corpses collected from
the swarmers, the wing drop. Wings everywhere.

Heard a pied butcher bird at the limit of its range –
pushing its voice and its geography, pushing
mimicry to undo the patterns embedded in your
memory. How many times have we heard the pied
butcher bird around here? Not that many, not really.
It covered the rufous whistler, grey shrike-thrush,
magpie, and approximated in a deeper voice, a gerygone!
The position of the sun in the sky – *sun path* – tilt –
arc – is the tuning fork which I notice is becoming
a characteristic of jam trees here – curved forks
enlichened, more than sharp isosceles, skinny triangles.
The curve that lures the pied butcher bird to test its range.

A pied butcher bird isn't a noun or an abstract noun.

Something scrabbling in the southwest corner
downpipe – a reptile unable to climb back up
to the gutter, the roof. Scrabbling. The only way

out, given the shiny interior's resistance to clawing,
is through the trap – the ground level outpipe
for debris. I open it to air, and even in heat, sludge
of the storms spills out. I hope the reptile will
find release, escape. Otherwise its death and rot
and into the Great Tank to disperse amongst
the house water. House we occupy. I am fairly
sure it's an ornate dragon, as we seem them rarely
here and another is on shadecloth near the wall,
just down from the roof. Offspring . . . partner?
Ornate dragons colour and blend, favouring granite.

An ornate dragon isn't a noun or an abstract noun.

And out there for a full viewing for first time
since days of storms after drought and then high
hot winds from the east, I am dismayed to the point
of agony to find five old York gums brought down –
two to the base, another falling and uprooting another,
all the small hollows characteristic of termite-eaten
old York gums torn apart, and owlet nightjars lost.
It is the collapse of a city, the changing of time signature
here – yet again, yet again in profound way but never
as profound as the slicing up into lots, the making
of 'Coondle', the fencing and 'opening' for livestock.
There is no post-trauma, it is ongoing, and this felling
by distressed nature, seems more than a caveat. Much more.
I cannot rewrite what has been rewritten, I am the vacancy
of a signature, an unofficial signing-off on the report?

A fallen York gum isn't a noun or an abstract noun.

Even out here it's hard to believe people speak
of those *'already* ill or old' being the bulk of the dead –
the hideous relegation of life to a table of stats,
to bracket creep of age. All roads lead to and from
a reassurance that consoles the numinous body,
the survivors, the Logan's Run futurism,
the jolt of social media and dislikes dislikes!

A person isn't a noun or an abstract noun.

How can any ode remain immune to what
is going on around it – the spread and the fear?
And to thwart anxiety the bluffers deploy 'panic'
as a weapon, as a tool of ostracism, rather
than working with empathy – take the
Easter Lilies risen after the storms, and the first
opening of this 'invader' fallen fast, neck broken
by weighty bird or roo hopping past, but still
searching for sun through the shade.
You could never set a clock by their appearance,
and now less than ever, but their appearance
shows the contra-indications of a chronology
imposed on the land as if it's immunity
to challenge, as if it was always going to be
this way – as if the Serenity Prayer
is the complete answer, whatever
the context. Don't worry, it stays
with me, but it's never infallible.

But I did notice in the warp of post-dawn,
the stats of cases of infection and bodycount
across the globe, a curve in the valley I'd never
really noticed before, and it was uplifting.
That an ongoing colonialism has bent ground
to its wants is not in question, but it's not recent,
though a firebreak has been carved through
the depression and its rise, but I feel the upraised
palm gesture laid bare by clearing is something
deeper and of greater duration in its making,
and says something beyond survey-husbandry
and is a guide more expressive and less prescriptive
than 'old-worldnew world' spatiality.
I pause and rest my gaze in the upturned palm,
the contour so close I had ignored without volition.

A person isn't a noun or an abstract noun.

An echidna has moved through and unearthed,
torn open, broken into the broken trees and dislodged
termite galleries, has supped deep into the dying trunks.
Earth is jumbled moist to dry and crumble and reset.
An echidna has moved through the wing-fallout,
traced and broken open, extracted, reset, terraformed.

An echidna isn't a noun or an abstract noun.

No Reflex in the making of this ark poem,
not moss quivering before the gnashing cut,
not now, but far back, or further back . . . but

[12]

pop-up forest in paddock already in agony
is different . . . different from (not 'to') old
growth persistence, distant, not seen out
this window and probably fewer and fewer
naturally occurring holes – tunnel vision
that blooms beyond cells in the human
brain, outside neural pathways, in the sap;
the resistance of moss on the ash trunk
in the growing realm of fire on fire on fire.
This intervention in composition, this drain
on power, this call for words fuelled as if
they answer and give more when they can't.
And I weep looking out – here at point
of composition – at the breakage
of old trees, the swathe angling down
valley, reconfiguring Jam Tree Gully
which is more than a concept,
it is an obligation, and thornbills
are the present continuous, the *ongoing*.

A forest isn't a noun or an abstract noun.

Out of the abuse and trauma and theft
and massacring you can't take on voices
of the dead the injured the hurt the affected:
it is not yours to document but to offer
restitution in material ways, maybe spiritual,
but not to write something you will benefit
from even if it's a, *Good on you for uttering
a truth*. Other voices have a right and a need

and you can listen, and act, but not tell.
Corrective stories still bristle wit story-
telling as if it's a way through: audience
says it can't be when that audience
sits back to read, sips on a drink,
takes in a sunset after placing a bookmark.

A people isn't a noun or an abstract noun.

Still the thornbills, still the seed gathers
gathering when the seed is thin on the ground
and some has sprouted after rains to die-off
in the new dry, barely beyond a low grass.
And now the mutations, the L-types and S-types
that are geographically inclined, demographically
requisite, their own little bigotry in sun and rain.
Here it has dried so quickly again, but thornbills
work together to gather, though at the end
of every moment of feeding action, it's their
own beak and their own beak alone that plucks
a particular seed from a cluster. This is no
analogy, no ontology, however much observation
pulls us that way especially when alone, isolated
or semi-isolated, holding what we have to hold.

And near the little finger of my left hand
as it acts to make letters – gentle strike of key
to type to shape words – I see written in thought
ahead of sight ahead of speech to erode a narrative
into an imaginary page . . . it is not real, not

really, is it? . . . near my little finger is the partial
silk-enwrapped shell of a 'swarmer', the vomited
on and broken-into corpse of a swarmer that kept its wings,
a small spider – hard to identify – upside down above it,
digesting, symptom of its symptom, refrain in the pulse
of my our-world, our collating of senses and recall
and loss – when termites swarmed over dry tracts
after sudden wet, after deluge, days and days ago
now, days back when this ode began and experience
could only fall away, unbalance, seed-twist
away from its cause, take root to pull up short.
And yet, the qualifiers are to be heard
and seen and sensed brushing the skin
if waited for – *sometimes, should, possible.*

Pasture Webworm and Pastoral Alarmism

Not frequent, the monitors of doomed pastoral
admit these native moths their autumn rising

after a sleepy eviscerated summer, stubble
suddenly alive with beakiness, and then and then . . .

emergence from pupae and the flutter the mating
and egg-laying that diagram of *cycle* leading

to larvae emergence – all these emergences
to dine on grass on young cereal crops on green blades

then setting shafts down into moist ground beneath
the succulent shadows under *under* to emerge *emerge*

at night in shadow in darkness under crescent moon
under moon in full bloom in raw starlight and to feed

to chew blades to feel the cold heat of dawn and retreat
into tunnels into shafts into burrows to seal to block

till next called on by night's growth-tricks the breath-ploys
and then emerge in a total way to emerge and stretch wings

and fly up through stubble to flay and lay and web with thread
the world against pastoral desiring and the cropping

and doom of agrichemicals, these 'native moths' adapting
to take in *nu-crop* spreading grasslands these alterities of fields

in patches here and there, the burnings and carbonisation
the charring the choking and the syllogisms of extinction

and that wing and that prayer and a topdressing
of faith and a *wistfulness* of pesticide and fertiliser

and bare bones watching closely should an infestation
emerge speak day into night survive the bloody georgic.

Eclogue of the New Vegetable Garden

PROLOGUE

The government would use us for mulch,
but this garden is veganic against the odds
they stack with denials and one step behind
the one exposed to what needn't have happened.
They say, 'We now have community spread . . . '
when fourteen days before the *now* was set in place.
They do not govern in the name of this gardener.
It is not a war. The *powers that be* think of all
as warfare – they treated fire as war, they treat
the virus as war, they play soldiers and kill us.

A GARDENER SPEAKS

The rocky ground can be but a bed to build on
but soil 'deposits' on rocky ground are hard to come by –
some yellow sand from an old building pile, white sand
from the arena, clay soil with leaf mulch from below
jam trees, forked and dug in and raised to a sky
Elon Musk keeps puncturing, usurping stars.

And the raising of fences to restrain rabbits
and roos, and the bricking around the bases of mesh
to stop the excavations, the underminings. But
in time of crisis when nurseries and seedbanks
are being stripped like supermarkets – country
supermarkets visited by city-dwellers who turn
visit into raid who affirm a government's language
of 'strip bare', giving the words to the very

powers that have let the anxious down, who
have raised the profiteers in their own image.
In such times, I search through boxes to find
four and ten and fourteen year old packets
of organic heirloom seeds, and these I sow.
Then racists kick in and blame 'foreigners'
or a particular community and the story
twists till it's all an urban myth served
best by the urban elites, by journalists
who can't nuance a story and say, It's
happened, and it's unfair to country people,
but racists have taken advantage of it to blame,
to create hatred towards innocent people.
In time of crisis, all subtlety goes out the door,
if ever it was there, and no comments sections
can save the decline of event and reality,
our virtual destruction of each other
to precede the final event, deaths
without funerals, lives stripped bare
and no 'hoards' of souls to call out, to accuse,
to sell off on stolen ground. The collapsing
narratives, the accusations flying in a wingless
world, and the air and ground and water
still being poisoned – locally. Terminologies
adapting to incorrect use, misinformation
to smother the misinformation. Loss.
    The collapse of world garden
at the behest of social media, gadgets.
Osmosis transpiration and breathing
are the ingredients of lockdown,

the deterrent but not pesticide: garlic,
chilli, vegetable oil, and a plant-based soap –
that will come into play, but not as a 'war'
against nature, but an interaction,
an encouragement to alternative paths.
Prediction? Foresight? Inevitability? Ah, the sun!

Rain was predicted but has been unpredicted,
the way of it since the centralising, the moving
of forecasting away from the local – the disrupted
weather speaking against the glib view of scrying.
Weather listens and responds to all and I am
hoping a microclimate will form around the metal
of the silver shed, will make signals with the old
wire fencing resurrected to protect the food
we will raise and share with older family
closed away in their isolation – they are
already excited by the photos. But water
is the issue, and we have so little flowing
or sitting, so little to prompt seeds
into a search for the fertile, so thin on here.

A garden map. Extensions planned to time
with the lowering sun, to fit the seasonal
brackets if not the degrading climate.
Marked out to be plotted filled in planted.
Rainfall permitting. Still some seed stock
if they're still able to germinate, unhollowed.
A garden map. A garden journal. A call
to Tracy to come out and take a look at how

it's going. And after lessons, Tim comes
out to help. This is where the cabbages
will rise from ash, where rocket is a journey
through biochemistry, soil unto body.

So what's *in*? Some of it 'out of season'
though seasons were never what they
wrote on the packet and are even less
so now, looking out of kilter as
the rapid change we've all made shifts
the planting guide . . . so what's *in*, now?
Well, what's available is what's *in*
and a risk has to be taken that the sun
will be played as length-of-day prompts
flowering and fruiting, though no doubt
as we fail to rise out of this crisis we'll
tilt the earth further to point of falling off?
But no, I have hope in the magpie carolling
and the thornbills' frenzied setting which
is pretty normal for them actually, even
if conditions have shifted and things
are tougher and the termites are stirring
beyond the echidna's capacity to survive
incursions, and silvereyes plan future
activities – no, not raids, all to be expected,
and not against the best possible outcomes,
not at all, this being for all, so build in
extractions even in time of dire need, stress.
So, tell us, what's *in*? Well . . . cabbages,
bok choy, silverbeet, chives, rocket,

bush beans, and late by any standards
but with hope . . . okra, aubergines,
and even a capsicum. More to come.
New beds planned . . . rocks lifted
and placed to make gentle walls
to hold back the roll of downfall
should it come again, should it come
again. Meagre water now. Sprinklings.

How many times I've dreamed this new
garden before beginning? – to grow
isolated with little water amidst rocks
with incisors and auxiliary incisors keen
to nip before the beds, to unroot to mock
the rhizome but make life which is incredible,
admirable, the essence of growth feeding
back into itself. How to grow out of contradictions.
How many times have I seen the layout
as manifested on the garden map,
in actuality around the silver shed,
likely first building when the surveyed-building
of factory materials intervened here
after the big land grant was broken up –
tin garden shed, then housepad, then kit home,
then two 'owners' on and we arrive, adding
on, extending, trying to grow broadbeans
on a fair scale in a harsh place. Back then.
Now the new garden, the garden of necessity
out of the disorder, the lies and threats
and inadequacies of governance, now

the love of umbrella anarchism and plants
grown from dust and moss and leaflitter.
And come next summer, once again
the acacia seeds will be ground as powder,
once again, as it was, and as it must be.

And now, in the now, if the now, and now
I just spritzed the garden with a little of our
water from the Great Tank, to coax and comfort
the seedlings and seeds, to give them and us hope –
contra-indicative and yet not, too, as 'to seed'
plants will be maintained to live their fullness,
for the seeds to be collected, next generation.
Some of our precious water – precious
has a meaning beyond quantifiable value,
and well beyond notions of 'property'. We only
have about three weeks supply left. If it doesn't rain
and there's no room in that estimate for watering
seeds and seedlings, for coaxing growth
against the new climate, the drought, the age.
Evening watering to retain moisture
after hot day. To make a brief highly
localised humidity. To conjure. A science.
And yes, mosquitoes in the ears, demi-contrary.

I go out to sustain using improvised
watering cans – water siphoned
from the eastern corner tank,
a small 2,000 litre two-thirds full
back up, and now the vegetables'

hope, or our hymn in this Grand Guignol
of pathetic fallacy I roll in like ash and dirt,
but try to work towards a 'pastoral ending',
peace at the end of the movement, or to restart
after the interlude, which is the only positive
that can be drawn from a pastoral on stolen land.
But I water and hope and when the times comes
from pollination, hope all the insects of here
will share in the unfamiliar familiarity – shape
their visions to suit our needs but lose none
of their intactness, their quiddity. Is this
possible? Is this the essence of the viral eclogue,
the movement towards post- in a hyper-damaged
ecology? I water with vats – top open for air-
flow to prevent vacuum as water pours
from punctures in the side – barely
deserving the term 'innovation', but needs
must, like lineation, and enjambment.

But what I see inside the fence are a pair
of joey tracks – small and sudden, as if
off track from the mob, quickly in and out.
A leaper, plus. I will have to make the fence
higher and even low fences feel so wrong.
I had positioned the new garden off the trails,
away from where the mobs move through,
had huddled in close to the silver tin shed,
an obstacle there's no getting around,
a glinting deterrent under even a part-moon,
with poor shine broken up by rainless clouds.

I am one step behind and need to move one ahead.
I water the prints into the soft, worked surface
under which the old seeds are either starting
to think a waking life or remain hulls emptied
of anima. A cautious watering, just enough,
a gauntness between dry and wet. Semi-elixir.

Insects are bucolic smashers built into a georgic
solution which will be garlic and peppers
with soap so it clings to leaves already grass-
hopped and the 'cabbage whites' are eyeing
a future which is completely understandable
but we have to work things out, don't we –
negotiate, discuss, displace and offer alternatives.
Yes, the rustle and shooshing sounds is me
talking with insects – listening, working out,
co-existing, loving and saying too much
is more than enough. Basil, marigolds,
garlic, mint . . . and any local deterrents
I can call from the crevices without wrecking
what few intactnesses of systems remain.
Eucalypt speaks loud and olfactory here, and I listen,
I listen, and know I can learn. Anew. Wings. Legs. Carapaces.

A Garden Speaks

It is easy for the eclogue to be let go –
a day missed-being-watered because reserves
are so low, and other factors intervening
from a world refusing then coming to grips
then refusing, convulsing locally and globally.
There was a global garden but it is fractured
now by globalism – gardens are so regional.
But they talk with each other, and pollen
travels so far. Already the birds and insects
are sniffing us out, testing soil and leaf,
waiting for the action. High and low
pressure cells converse and we wave
to each other, cross-species, huddled together
in patches and rows and, gratefully,
mixed together. But a light sprinkle
comes and along the barriers snow pea
and French bean seeds are sown, and then more
water comes. Not a torrent, but enough for
us all to keep going, gasp a little less,
keep our vasculars pumping, keep
the light sourcing and changing.
Our photographing of self
came long before, and is life-giving.
That some seed is plucked by a thornbill
beak of seed clarity is part and parcel
but who's saying it wants to be me or more,
this bizarre pact of giving as mistranslated
by people, but let's call it a kind of symbiosis,

a kind of system closed or open that gives
life a chance. French beans – don't think
for a moment we don't care about origins
and where we are planted and how we grow
and why. And the fates and suffering,
and richness and barrenness. All caught
inside the eclogue, our hope of liberty?

A GARDENER SPEAKS

Seriously gardening – gardening seriously –
leaves little room for much else. It's an obsession
of survival for others, not just the self. Honestly.
And there's no ill-wind tone in this, no leaf blight,
no photoshopping of the bounty, the dying leaves,
the vulnerability. So punnets are made for an elder
to pick up, and some small packets of heirloom
seeds from the meagre stockpile (but lucky – surprise
discovery in a cardboard box! this is the refrain –
a prospect of germination of harvest of next
generations), for him to plant away from here –
back-up for all of us, different soil different conditions
and much more water on tap, the grand hope
under the mountain but beyond the shadow
which is no bad thing in itself, but of properties
beyond the scope of a garden, but not the roots, rhizomes.
Over there, barn owls and bats over-view in March nights.

It's hard to think beyond the garden because it's essential
we think inside the garden, watch over with stretched arms,
bent backs, *eye* in the back of our *head*, but all senses alive.
Some gardening can take place in darkness and silence.
Magpies keep track and trace their presence around
    cultivars.
As daylight closes to magenta and valley peaks lock
out the last sunrays, we know a different growing
will be done, our breaths taken in and healed,
but when sunrise comes a new process begins
and we are entirely part of that too. Respirators.

I am shocked in the garden not by the exquisite
blue butterfly which will investigate the plants
to lay to elicit the first instar to call ants to suggest
ants are at their beck and call but it's mutual,
but this is not shock it is pattern the shock
is hearing of the Texan Lieutenant governor saying
generations of 'old people' would be sure to want
to give up their lives as sacrifice for a 'strong economy'
for the young. Out of this grotesque inversion
of the usual war talk in all this militarising
of sickness and response, I hear the asparagus
crowns rising to full-strength in the grounds
beyond the porch of the house where Tim came
home from being birthed in Columbus, home
to rural Gambier where many gardens awaited
their time. I think of that from this new garden
in ancient soil at Jam Tree Gully, and of the gall
of that Governor, and his trickle down of greed

to breed strains of rapacity for generations
to the very end, till the last harvest, the last seed.
I am shocked in the garden not by the exquisite
blue butterfly, but what's beyond the garden
and its undoings and redoings, its awkward
acclimatising, barometer of hungry and thirsty
leaves, curling yellow, driving new green. *Esse*!

A Garden Speaks

As definite as the article is hope is prospect
I might nurture. Today I have extended myself –
a new bed but not bed of roses, no place
to rest. This gravelly clay mixed with building
sand from the house extension a decade ago,
worked through with leaf litter – doesn't
promise much now, but it might later, in whatever
later I manifest, osmosis of soil and air, and,
when it arrives, the rain, the runnels and gouges
of erosion, the random deposits of seed to latch
on to old work and much older patterns, to rise
against the megrims, the midpoint of a hillside.
It is eruptive, and sounds almost gross, but it's
a joy, actually. Even if this fails something
will eventuate, form in the nurseries of dirt.
I wonder if those who turn up their noses
at turnip soup or more beetroot than a garnish,
will find stories of food and feeding that are
taken for granted, brought in from seedbanks.
Sounds. Maybe the last strains of 'Purple Haze'

shimmering mirage-like over me, us, this promise
of sap, electricity of rhizomes, leaf, stalk, taproot.

A GARDENER SIGNS OFF FOR THE TIME BEING

Compost is gravel-ant time – intense as refusal,
of swarm that isn't metaphor or symbol or double-
edged outside the pincering of 'angry ants', which
they're not, particularly, but they mean what they bite.
And top-dressing with sand from the old horse arena
which was a vision of training winners, of triumph
in the ring – I have no idea if it proved so or not.
But the sand will top-dress the garden and counter
time of spread and quarantine and lock down
and social isolation and the freaky yoking of denial
and risk and biosphere and recuperation and benevolence
which is the bounty of new growth and regrowth
and preservation and conservation and veneration.

Eclogue of the Gardener and the Pastoral Elegist

GARDENER

I transferred a small wood scorpion
from the kitchen sink draining board
to the vegetable garden where it slip-
streamed into dryish mulch strewn
below leafy greens, semi trapping
the moisture from bare bones watering.
What are the ethics of this? My role,
it's displacement, but not far from
its origins, and maybe really close.
Some parts of leaf have been eaten
to gridwork, but yesterday a potion
of cayenne pepper and garlic powder
warded off and discouraged, as vinegar
by the litre (in short supply) and cayenne
deterred the furiously burrowing rabbits
housing by undermining our housepad.
Us and them, ours and theirs. Truisms.

The old expired heirloom seeds have failed
to find inner resources beyond their biology,
to construct life without the systems being
intact, in place. I believed they'd find a way
through deterioration to an essence of growth,
a desire to reach for the sun, to maybe
be desultory at first, but defy the breakdown
since their formation, their drying off
and collection and storage, their before
expiry date enthusiasm to unleash life,

to get going. But other than the radishes,
no, all have stayed silent, or broken down
further with that racket of merging but not
the sonorous pushings aside of emergence.
But I am not completely sure as some might
have made it through and been eaten by insects,
or cut in the soul by cutworm – there are possibilities
of exception to the general pattern, the observable
trends.

       So, I prepare half a dozen punnets
of varying sizes and plant old seeds of different
species and varieties to see what comes of it –
an experiment in controls, in measurement
of prospects, in boons of life and decay
and of what point they are and we are
in relationship to their trajectories.

Yes, there are birds in the sun in the seed;
birds I am listening I am hearing the germ
of the sun-seed; birds of the sun are dipping
in around me, splinters of fire on the edge
of fire season, alarm that offsets so much,
but cooler nights mean some safety. I wonder
if the owlet nightjars hunt insects at night
in the garden? I look out for their droppings –
scry the upturned soil as I water the punnets.
I have set the control. I hear a soundtrack
outside copyright in the freakout residues.
Okra is the tallest tower in the garden

but sunflower is fast overtaking in this
realignment of seasons from six to two.
Hot and cool. I will dream I am watching
an okra plant as the fixed camera watched
the Empire State Building from the window
of the Time building. As sunset's requiem
is the wink of lights going out, the flashes
and cauterisations of time. That city I love
as if it was nature and not against nature.
I think of Jonas Mekas's *Walden* as notion
of nature-life in city context requiem we
are less separated than some might think?
He cites Andy's question: 'What is action?'
How implicated in fascism was Jonas?
How does a *position* shift with geography?
Action is an underground aphorism of cutworms
of time open ended but closed as offices
of flower-urging wink out star-effect here
to track constellations blink floodlit timing,
night held back from light-tower observation
top storeys bush clutching garden here
not one and the same – no pan pipes
for pan who stays seated chatting till
reflected in window's changing spools
every half an hour or so as fixed as two
lights at 45 degrees to each other to code
the euphony of sleep perchance fountain
light of spent seed city steel and as sun sets
the truth is told and clouds fly past fast
or slow as fast-slow birds and now only

one or two 'mercy flights' left to go out
overhead, arcing across the restricting
access the switch flicked like the silvereye
wing-flipping a leaf and the punnets
set not far from the spire of okra. Sleep.

PASTORAL ELEGIST

I resow rows of failed seeds with the few
'in code' packets of organics I have – closed
off from supply . . . onions, cauliflowers,
silverbeet, sweet basal and a few sunflowers
to temper the soil at the edges. And then,
a honeyeater I've not seen around – such
irruptions happen occasionally, especially
as climate shifts and breaks down trying
to compensate for the damage, telling
us that to be anthropomorphised is
the least of its problems, and that it would
expect no more than this given the human
interference. This honeyeater is from
around the 'Swan River' – the colonised riverspace
that is older than maps of conquest, much
much older, and in the dry space of here
where there's a watering-can maintenance
of garden, it twitches and sings smaller
bursts than it might, anxious over the little
water falling on leaves, channelling
to roots. Western white-naped honeyeater –
Gould in the mid-nineteenth century

decided it might be called Gilbert's
honey-eater, unable to hear in its song
an exchange of name of bird to human
and human to bird that had gone on for
a comparative 'forever'. But here it is
temporarily inland at least, up from the dry
brook, the low river down to the sea-fed
lower reaches where volume is still held.
This aftermath of its breeding season,
though who's to say now, searching
older ground for a mate out of its heyday.

And as a pair of yellow-plumed honeyeaters
flicker around the lessening leak in the Great Tank
(the level on an edge now, the meniscus
collapsing in on itself), enravelling with frantic
silvereyes, news reports swirl with the felling of millions
of poplar trees in Kashmir because of 'seasonal
allergens' and anti-Covid tactics to prevent
coughing and sneezing and spread of the virus.
Yes, the trees will pay. Yes, the heating will
continue though industry has been cranked
back . . .' but the furnaces won't crack, and industry
has an eye to a futureless future, a compulsion
to see us through to the end it underwrites.
The garden wants many ends that don't align
with our vision of a transpirational deliverance.
I am hearing Peter Tosh and am connected
though I gave up smoking weed quarter
of a century ago – now I sing elegies

of life, of life from the ash to grow from.
No ground zero, only the infinite prospect.

GARDENER

Watering ancient seeds that will never appear
with the little water available. But I have unearthed
a couple of packets of old lettuce seeds and I have
a hunch a premonition a strong feeling a hope
that this will be a eureka moment against
the evisceration the drying the emptying-out
of life over time. I have a feeling they will
buzz like the radishes and germinate and grow
and grow and love all weathers towards sustaining
themselves and us. Lettuce is my hope my oracle
my celebration against the prevalence of elegy!
Tomorrow will be a getting filthy day
a getting into the profile of soil
to liberate to lay down hope. Arise!

PASTORAL ELEGIST

You lie awake night after night
your life insomnia eating life via
faux time spent conscious but you
gain nothing more thinking is done
in rapid eye movement near the lidded
surface and even in furrows of deepest sleep.
Awake, fretting, worrying about the distance
between rows between plants,

the optimals. Such a desperate
plea, avoidance of verisimilitude,
as if you're making a story
you can fit into, control.
Lamentable. A dry dirge.
Mistaking a noxious 'weed'
for a hoped for cultivar,
you nurture disappointment,
the limbo beyond insomnia.
Nightshade seedlings look so
like the out-of-date Jalapenos
don't they, don't they? I sow
doubt into your sleep deprivation,
dirty fingernails inside gloves
that keep nothing out, not really,
the tongue of earth flapping
without speech – frenulum
of sunflower that's lost its head,
dividing you and me at the hinge.

GARDENER

The proverbial (actually, barely that now) three drops of rain
fell on me while I was filling the watering can from the last
two-hundred litres remaining in the 'spare' water tank. It
wasn't 'like' sarcasm, it was sarcasm. In the hope of a fall,
I transplanted onion and cauliflower seedlings, thinking
a better life awaited them in the prepared bed, though they
could sustain in their pots for another couple of weeks
with far less water. A risk taken and now evisceration.

I wonder if Trent Reznor making 'a copy of a' had any
notion of the reach, the dust-depth of this dry, its copyism
of vestiges of life, the root sent out, searching but left stranded,
not even breaching the outer layer, the roof of the underworld?
This is nothing to do with a 'battle', it is to do with antonyms,
to do with love of growth, of all that it needs to find a way through.
Did I see a silvereye poke a seedling into the ground, to secure
its roots better than I had secured them in their en-soiled bundle?
I believe I did, I am sure I did, this mutual aid this colloquy.

PASTORAL ELEGIST
for Ouyang Yu

Each effort made
thwarted – a flick
of denuded soil
into our face, roots
of a wild oat entangled
through the roots
of a cabbage just
getting going – separation
bringing both to grief,
and you. Those greens
that urge you to pick them,
the first yellow flowers
appearing before the plants
have had the run they
would desire in an ideal
world, following
the almanac, the planting

guide, the phases
of the moon, the tilt
of a sun transported
across hemispheres,
the politics of
acclimatisation.
Today – overcast –
new insects are vigorous,
and why wouldn't they be,
cutting leaves down
to size – amplitude
of all spirit you invest,
your fascination
with poems
of stillness:
静 . . . ? I hope
you will learn,
will listen, will
value. Taking
a plant to make
connection, to think
over the thousands
of poems you have read,
your intrinsic interest
in flood and mist,
gardens of the flood-
plains. Can you take
that inside with you,
remember it without
making it part

of your body?
It will grow in you
as it can't grow
to its fullness outdoors,
in the conditions.

GARDENER

The sun is whiteout in oversupply to the grid,
and the irony leaves me searching for colours
of health in the leaves. A mosquito bites my arm
and I can't resist, I must let it do so, within
the confines, the infinite expanse, of the garden.

PASTORAL ELEGIST

You need to talk
about your successes
and failures bringing
food to our mouths,
bringing poems to our
senses, recording
the atmospheric
disaffections,
the particulars
of soil and moisture.
The lacks. The spiritual
increase that isn't balance.
And now more test
punnets, more hope

all seeds will sink
through the ground
and not float
hollow, birds
turning away.

GARDENER

Persistence is the remonstration
of song – so I go inside and eat
canned pears dished up lovingly
with a sweet sauce out of the limits,
the frugal times. We talk of trees
laden with new ripening pears
seen a couple of months ago
before the regional shutdowns,
over the line where we don't go now.
On the road's edge; we wonder
if someone picked them, and
served them up with an idea
of bolstering against future
scarcity. Each year's crop
wondrous as the next
should it make it through,
when time, as Cressida says,
'is old and hath forgot itself . . .'

Eclogue of It Having Rained Overnight

'you will find me if you want me in the garden
unless it's pouring down with rain'
BLIXA BARGELD

GARDEN

It has rained overnight – not a lot,
but enough to touch below the surface-layer,
tempt or taunt or soothe the subsoil. A deeper
quenching than any the gardener
has been able to give us. His giving voice
is a ploy as we are prepped to his end,
an end in which only some of us will see
our way through to seed, the gestural
hibernation, the activism of prayer-time.
Ask yourself what you are doing
to the collective body and soul
as well as each angle of sustenance,
each propagation towards an organic
    cosmology, that before and during
the first instant, it was all root, rhizome, tendril.

GARDENER

What leaves the bounds of protection –
the fence against foragers and diggers –
is to be celebrated, and I wish it well
where it doesn't choke out others.
This puts me in a position of responsibility
and sunders your agency, which is either
hypocrisy or paradox of physiology.

GARDEN

I fool you – I only want growth
to maximal effect, and *growth*
isn't necessarily what you desire, what
you have in mind. I throw up so many
deceptions which ethics tells you can't
be thought of as such – I taunt you
with plants you can't possibly
let run their course. Dilemma?

And that rain shower, what are
its implications beyond a day or two?
Many, I tell you. Different birds
have arrived and certain insects
have switched into next stages,
different predations and ingestions.
But it's also the optimism of rise,
of stretch, of loving the sun
you have so come to fear
when it works on a different
time-scale from your despoliations.
You have refocussed it, but I – we –
search it out through the lens
of cloud tracking its halo,
find heat in gravity
nurturing. We're not
giving up the code yet,
no matter how much the esurient
'knowledge seekers' try to unravel

us, reduce us to nuts and bolts.
At least you admit none of them
by choice. At least. We share
    that resistance,
by what we *apportion* in austerity?

I have a report of potatoes
reaching up from their hollows,
waiting to be covered layer by layer,
but not here, not yet. Too dry.
This little rain won't reach
them in their heart of hearts.
Not yet. But as you say, optimism!

We can feel the diggings – the vibrations
of tunnelling and flicking out sand and clay –
they find the softer places we aren't given
access to – they dig into your 'forbidden',
these rabbits edgy with drought, furiously
searching for places to birth under trees
that are drought-tolerant dying dying.

All those schemes you have – the cayenne
and vinegar, the disturbing entries and exits –
put to the test at a time of stress. You'd expect
us to support your vision, but for all your

veganics, we'd add lustre to our growth
if our roots tapped blood and bone
like your grandfather spread in sackloads.

GARDENER

He did. And he told me as a child to smell it,
all that growth, he said, that goodness, but
I knew it a haunting from the family tales
of his falling into the offal pit at Benny's Bone Mill,
and that he couldn't stand the site of the uncooked,
and wanted his dead flesh burnt to a crisp.
He counteracted his anxiety with blood and bone –
death outside of recognition, ebullient growth,
garden in raptures to the strains of piano,
violin, euphonium, the brass band he played in,
green thumbs on the brass valves, 'sweet voiced'.
But you, dear garden, in your dusty realm,
your sensitivity to subterranean acts,
will grow from the sheddings of your own,
unless a bird perches, eats, and shits – fine, fine!

GARDEN

Constraint and restraint and dependence.
Not GM or hybridising or messing with our
essence, but we are variables and beholden
to your whims and needs. Even our celerity
if fed and watered is pulled back, to grow

at a pace of your desiring. It's you messing
with 'nature's gap' to play out your drama.

GARDENER

See the female red-capped robin curving
its wings – run, curve wings out as if to wrap,
then flap and run, gather materials for a nest –
early if so, very early, but dry is compulsion
and seasonal switch – six – four – two –
one blow of dried leaves of acacia acuminata
to catch in a beak and run arch run. Not display.
Not antics. Ritual and knowledge and more.
Not mutually exclusive, and alongside the garden.

GARDEN

The garden. An article. Property per the denial
of property? Slipshod. Winds lifting and smoke
building, smothering – the degenerative burn-offs.
The fixed point of the recidivists is at time of crisis
to keep the demi-old Euro farming ways in full
swing – fire meets fire and quenches the lack?
I see you choking up – it's not me alone
that . . . precipitates . . . your hayfever, the failure
of etymology because it sounds like a plague
of insects sweeping in before I have risen.

GARDENER

It is dusk and yet the fantails unmask
themselves along with red-capped robin
to pick mosquitoes and gnats and late
flying ants from your troposphere,
to change with specificity that which you
encourage. I see this, and vicinage
works propinquity and I allow
that I am almost a plaything
and not. This elevation
to catch the sun halo the hills.

GARDEN

Last words, requiems, elegies.
What you don't know set
against all you want to know –
your records, your maps, your
declarations against secrecy;
but at least this is not
the fallout zone of many
of our confréres, consœur . . .
colleagues. This open secrets act,
this defiance *if not breaking*
of drought, our folioles of doubt.

Sub-Eclogue

Back from the world,
the interlocutor laments
the lack of anything
'garden' left on shelves –
all to do with vegetable-
raising stripped bare,
other than three packets
of dwarf beans to be sown
no later than late summer.
But mid-Autumn and it's
still warm – hot for the time
of year – so needs must.
Growth now is a change
of variables that makes
the equation harder,
not easier. Beans
will be planted,
at least their germination
likely – some kind of journey
if not destiny. Even hope
is reconfigured, listening
to Hadyn's *The Creation*:
Raphael so low in subsoil
he heals the room for roots
to tap into, illustrate,
as they might rise
to sing atmosphere.
We are already far

too far beyond
a prelude.

GARDEN

Inland you'd treat
me with seaweed –
a dousing that could
rouse iodine to fuel
a frantic reaction,
hormone of earthiness,
body's redress
soprano daylight
as Gabriel is messenger
of shared fertility,
androgynous love
of pure growth.

Neoterics and The Field (out of Callimachus)

No walking ground the same
no matter what there'll be
in adjustments.

This oven this earth as dust this water we watch vanish and ancient
is added to a list of household items swapped when worn out
for shoes that light-up walking the fence-lines, those boundaries.

The sharp-toothed dog on the hill is fenced-in. The echidna
in the rocks below sets out at dusk to roll across the hills basically
unchecked in its flightpath, but vulnerable to a leap of the fence, to tearing
   jaws.

Callimachus and Apollonius of Rhodes (he's back now with a polished
and bolstered version in-hand), know the properties of papyrus
beyond its worth in song.

Which part of the night sky I see, you see; we share without having to cast
contrails as locks where we can't go for all science's wish-fulfilment
sacrificing to show what's between thought bubbles.

The sun has been so bitter I doubt there's anything narcotic
or even soporific left in dried cells' thin walls of grass and wildflowers
to change desire lines of sheep, their groundart so resoundingly pragmatic.

It is difficult almost impossible to set a route through the haze
of bush-clearing dust or the abrasive pluming of a spark
as carbon-release, the emptying out of the sink.

The chilliest twenty-four hours were those of translation-loss
beneath a sun whose rays reached the earth so fast and so strong
they curled paper before you could sign off on the data.

625: Where the flock filed between manna wattle saplings you'd expect
big damage, but there was no ruse large or small, just a passage
away from the stranger.

The writing-surface was intended to decay and fragment in this way –
what you now read is what was intended to be read, what has gone was
    never
meant for your eyes at the time in these places.

The Extractor-in-Chief of iron-ore has a waterslide from the crown of his
    yacht
to the point just before breakers start to lift – later, scientists from his
    university
will haunt his sport, stare into oracular swirls of micro-plastics.

These inland thoughts
on a fiercely hot and dangerous day – exhausted
even before dawn fell.

Eclogue of a Catalan Farm in Time of Crisis

for Maria and Brian

Ash tree *answers* and asks its own questions
on the edge of the barley crop, those rows
of trust, that green preventative as lichen
holds tiled shed in place holds roof
as roof, and I walked there, too.
Let's start with the beauty that's skewed
so we can see the ethos of what persists –
the crux, the essence, the kernel.
Let's celebrate and then consider
what holds the core in place,
insists it behaves according to mandate.
Eclogue is memory's selection
of bucolic collapse where nothing
was ever perfect but is stressed
to edges the ash tree can't watch over,
act sentinel, where herbicides will clip
a pathway, a separation. Ideals selected.
Gendered as powerlines, as concrete
pads to build on – the raising green
houses and dwellings, ash tree's
century of witness. Easy and hard
as that. Hard as trying to find translations
into English of the poetry of Rosa Leveroni
or, say, Ana María Martínez Sagi,
though I find a reading of Leveroni's
haiku that begins: 'Com l'ametller florit'
that is so beautiful that it slips from its context
into the kernel of *the* farm, the garden,
the journey just beyond Lleida, spread across

a family, side by side, olive-tree-grip
and the grape giving and other fruits,
and I think, the world shares not takes,
for all the agonies imposed, the rights
stripped away; what you see from a tower,
what you hear over the plain, from
the sepulchres far out of visibility
up on the rock, the blur of the Segre
splitting city bridge with borderline
silence till flood isolates with similitude.
These conventions of empires and conquest
and versions of oppression gardens
might grow against – and out of – resuscitating
stillness and silence into activity, liberty, peace.
A green olive fruit purples in gesture,
to cluster towards health of community.
The sky is brine but looks magnificent –
overcast heft broods more than God,
more than ripeness, more than cataclysm,
more than seasons can turn, as lawn mown
to rise from sand from soil to grasp
its calenture, a hay cart brought
down from mountains for repair.
What refuge could I find crossing
such mountains, specific as people?

So, this is me processing what you sent
as photographs of where I had been with you –
a guest – decades ago, to replay against
alteration, maybe fluctuation of sap

and roots and stem and branch and age;
I know the paths of pines and ditches
and walls being able to say, *I was there*,
and here I know as I look out across
a valley of inference, of change that has
broken and been rearranged, and still
deep-rooted trees and annuals surviving
the blast remain, just, but I plant
around them. Yes, three pines –
they age well. They bristle with retrospect
and verticals, with aspiration and steadfastness.
Fallout is survived by them. No track
that passes them can be capricious.
And looking out, further and into
the 'depression', the orchards of blaze,
the peach blossom overload that costs,
too, as beauty always does when
aligned with the eye's needs, desires.
Each tree's V of spray the paradox
of representation, as if the flowering
is real, even hyperreal. *Listen*, singers.
Agriculture is the cost of eclogues
and you can get lost in the competition
of voices, the shared market in which
some rise and fall and rise and fall.
Trails pass wilder ground and waver,
determined to be steady towards productivity.
But a peach tree – a single peach tree –
in Salvador's orchard is a revelation –
an absolution, a free radical, a glory

beyond any grotesque gain-of-function,
any research into better beauty or horror.
Fruit will set if the flowers are loved
and let follow their lines to fulfilment.
Small-scale versus the industrial.
Salvador's orchard links hands
with the farm, and offers apple blossom
as well, and it enriches the sky – antennae,
cupola, colours beyond the spectrum:
mixed metaphors we rely on to see.
In flowerings no one hides behind
rituals of reproduction – it's effusion
and plethora! As usual, I had a sleepless
night and tried to think an infusion
of camomile to escape the rules of a
horticulture I grow against – wanting
to be *in* the germination, the emergence,
the urge towards seeing, the death
that is no death as flowers then fruits set,
seed falls to grow again. But soil is inconsistent,
and really I want sleep to detoxify. Like sunflowers.
Let the hills bandy about light, toss terms
like *sunrise* and *sunset* to all-consuming night.
Let the violets distract and mislead us,
let the tall, sharp stork work the grass
before the solar panels have collated the day,
let Sisqueta and Tonet, Salvador, Montse,
Albert and Joan, and Brian, Edmund and Maria
live next to each other for as long as land is land,
as long as the garden nurtures an energy

beyond power plants and satellites,
and longer, much *much* longer, still –
simultaneous, parallel, co-existent
as best suits their needs, their similarities
and differences – each room
planted with barley or maize
and a good neighbour looking on
as the mower keeps the grass trim but edgy.
Compost, terracotta, bursts of *Spartium junceum* –
'ginesta' which I won't dance because
I like to think I don't *take*, but I celebrate
in the circuits of voices, the hands to hands
of safer times, that will come again –
sardana! Step jump step! And the colour
calls us to its display – insects frantic
for continuance. *Curts curts llargs llargs . . .*
Don't think I ever forget the music
of the light breeze passing through
as I passed under the pines. The essence
of crops and labour, the contradictions
of immersion, lost alone and finding others
there, too. Easy, easy, not too fast. Ebullience.
Each room each patch each field each zone.
Even dry years and drier years to come
will implode the contradictions of oleander
in full flower, the key to the anti-garden,
anterior point of entry to the vegetal,
an aside to roots' pivot and hold. *Poisonous?*
Lavender and light, hay cart, a bloody
old olive tree that dares us to reassess

presence, persistence, reliability. Yes!
Touch the bark and blow on the leaves.
Olive trees are the stacks of renewable
industry like no other – factory emissions
are mocked by them, not the other way
around. Love and fealty are complex.
The reach of succulents and drainage
to take away the hopes, the watering –
which here – from where I write from memory
and correspondence, from a construction
of images – terms drainage a sarcasm,
the rain that won't come, the tanks
that won't fill, the subterranean plenty
that is contaminated then vanquished.
We share a hope for water, for flow,
across the vastness, the curvature.
Here, seed and garden companies can't cope
with the sudden rush of demand –
survivalism and cultivation linking hands,
and rainmakers are called out ahead of bushfires,
a season closer each year of a damaged
calendar. Against inevitability, I truly wish
you there – all of you there – a better
unfolding of a hurt year, a recovery from the loss,
from pastoral elegy. Ash tree *answers* and asks
its own questions – I know lichen here as I might
   know lichen there. I send this
   over the edge of day.

Eclogue of Grantchester Garden

for John Kerrigan

Who tells the story asleep in memory
to be stirred by distress by the division
of hemispheres the mirror blinding
as the sun rises into an overly warm day –
the antibodies of meadow and stile,
of *Lonicera nitida* hedge of apple tree
in rampant bloom to adapt or defy?
And so the gene-tampering companies
hide (or hid and will hide, still, again,
flowing towards . . . source . . . on . . . Great Ouse . . .
Wash . . . port gates . . . North Sea . . . platforming . . .)
behind the glistening buds then unfurling *sudden*;
or did, once, in *older days* enhancing
the new with seed not planted but strewn
unless planted in keeping with *futurity's* patents,
with co-operation and mutual interests,
contra old ways of old voices that renew
but aren't heard – which is not to say
they are pure or virtuous, but also
not to say they're not; rejoice in having
admitted new community, a co-existence,
which is welcomed in the telling of local stories
which are stories of growth in all localities
without being ruinous to those localities.
So unloosed, we tell the story of humanity
and grain, and wonder over happy herds
and their moderators. Let's, for a moment,
separate Ruskin (a 'type' of sheep), say,
from what he's viewing (a vegetal scene),

his intellectual copyright of calyx and skin
and flowering body parts – poise, imptetus.
This is no Brexit zone, no right of way
with a profiling – all can pass, can
take in the songs of blue tits and robins
because blue tits and robins say so,
and unstress fallacy because they
have their record-keeping, their
scaling your house wall trellis, the creeper,
the fumes of seed rape on quiet
roads. We can lose ourselves in this,
in the sheer ebullient contradictions of sustenance
and visual adoration and 'productivity' and, don't
forget, labour – the dirt and tired limbs
for all the machinery and GPS notation.
The five bar gate beyond the Blue Ball
is the route near and far, beyond and within,
I took to find a way through and from,
a set of steps familiar to residents
who say home is breath, and no breath
is stolen – it is the gift. I count every
blossom offered in the painting,
the moment that ever and never was,
the fixed expression in the tableau
vivant which can and can't belong.
Move, shape, look, hold. Represent.

We discuss this hearing the stories:
strong and disturbing, as yielding
to song wherever song has come

from. That trick of respect and distance,
of welcome and isolation. Each visit
each performance witnessed in orchards
in gardens on the paths along the old
river where brimstone butterflies 'cavort'
and struggle with pronouns, where
the preterite dominates a vanishing
tense of presence, and 'prudence'
is a research topic. I knit the weather
from muddy steps, from cow dung
dust which makes a low atmosphere
for gnats, the river's offsprings
no matter the stress, but they too
could vanish. In the heart of the blasted
willow are footholds that five way,
add a fertility that misses its codes,
information artefact, design manoeuvres –
in the return to soil what particulate
can hold, the smog in the glade?
The anglers manipulate water
and stock with stolen goods. Dumped.

But stories are vital and generative as well,
and such ground can hold the patterns
of growth and welcome attempts to rehabilitate –
there is no 'too late', as the players
try another angle to make the desired
picture. Vivant! Each blossom counted,
and each grain of pollen counted, and each
insect hidden in the mass of pink and white and red

and green, brought into focus. Reinstated.

In this calyx of words, the parity of plant
tissue and flesh, of the fusion *researchers*
try to imitate then patent – as if they own
the stories. They don't. The immensity
of gesture is the garden enclosure
palpated into lights – *this* light, here,
that light, there. And there and there.
Such mapping closing in on the problem,
on the domain we speak through – so
much quarantine, so much distance,
and yet, fumingly close, the seasonal
irritations ignoring the failure of seasons.
Remember, though a ride – a lift –
is always on offer, I have to find my
own way there, navigating by hedge
and asphalt that's giving way, negated
and spurred on by magpie and blackbird,
and yes, yes, the pheasant that makes
purpose outside its contingencies
in the divvying up of land, the apportioning
and profiteering, the bills of lading.

And in this, we meet in full agreement,
the *actual* being the beauty where beauty
is a lie of the tableau, an art of forgery –
they are nothing compared with hospitality,
your gifts in the garden read in strains
of shade – *in* the hedge and apple blossom,

in the grasslands and chalk and clay,
what emerges from silts beyond
farm discharges and residues
of mobility, vole and kingfisher
still work out what they can
of the mutable, and the pike's
theorem of sleep and mayflies
as if all was in place in the apparatus
of codex and witness and the garden's
body clock the sun falling down
and I wait to hear that we
can see it coming up the other side
of the enclosure, the garden, the wilds?

Eclogue of the Garden Pheonix

'From this session interdict
Every fowl of tyrant wing,
Save the eagle, feather'd king;
Keep the obsequy so strict.'

WILLIAM SHAKESPEARE

That mood can so inflect the garden
inflects, drags you into the prisms.
of the house, and even the garden
verandah light on, and a massive
and shook leaves with feathers
I know it was a barn owl for though
of night around here moves like that
don't hunt that way. I disturbed
'The Phoenix and the Turtle'
make you hesitate before stepping
In guilt of presence shades stir.
caught around the window lit
pellets after the morning watering,
would never mock the garden,
taste, unless they get desperate,
I tell them that these seeds are true
they are vulnerable to the exposure
the hybrid ploy of disease resistance,
But 'true to parents' and 'true to type'
and dragged out of the enclosure,
Garden is where soul is tested
recover from' accruals disperse
the exception that you fear will
in a rush to get to end's new beginning.
with anguish and second-guessing.
as affection for any growth confuses

as precious water on precious leaves
Last night, a tread in the air and a beating
trembled. I went out into the dark,
barn owl spread shadow wings
and arced down into the valley.
its face was hidden from me, no bird
and eagles don't fly at night,
myself with lines from Shakespeare's
because unfamiliar night sounds
into darkness. Isolation swerves.
Atlas moths – not their naming –
by a movie. I search for owl
and bronzewings tell me they
that the seed I plant is not to their
adding the wise caveat that they might.
to themselves and true to us, too –
of here out of place, and don't carry
of better and stronger and dead-ended.
are verbal tools of gardening realities,
we need to be wary how they grow.
garden is where the 'I will never
with pollen from a bolting exception,
become the norm, the whole crop
That's open pollinated overwritten
No F1 hybrids to distract your cause
pictures of purity – love the creation

for itself, not its origins. But I obsess
and degrees of mutability. And I fear
philosophies that arise from analogies.
or flower no matter what, I will find
policies, the defiance of husbandry.
given laid out waiting to be spoiled,
the mushroom cloud we archive
version of creation or apocalypse,
a graphing of imagination's limits,
stretching and curving and planting
year's beans and peas were and moving
getting a long-term grip, and glorious
that the only manures in my fallows
and drought, which fallows its lexicon.
a possible future, a pseudo-plenty
of subtexts and echoes. I cannot
myself why the dry-seeded paddocks
urgent beds of green upstarts? This
of the tractor driver, air-seeder throwing
evocation of fire in dust, the ash
around each specimen – votive,
that yield a compost pit at best,
accumulated across
agriculture – 'a poor harvest' –

over prehistory and cause and effect
the abuses of genetics, the social
I will love the reaching root, leaf
relief in growth escaped from containment
The stale historicising of gardens
the nuclear flowers aching underground,
as frontispiece or plates for an illustrated
as if it's a loop, a doughnut, a pretzel,
disembarking from the point to point,
nitrogen-hungry plants where last
crops to avoid 'pests' (those nematodes!)
fallow of the strip system except
are bird and insect and reptile droppings
But I am looking ahead – gleaning
to emulate the sun in these plantings
find an owl pellet. I cannot ask
across the valley seem to stare at these
feeding thing this emotional starvation
up a dust storm, the stomach-churning
from last 'winter' I sprinkle
oracular, offerings to the self
or wither away into stats
a century of invasive
to live to die to live by?

Garden Eclogue: binary interstices

'More to pollen ascript for elated finish'
J. H. PRYNNE

o

All these gardens conspiring to feed
and breathe world out of the land grant
militarism reward sequencing of global
conflict and landlordism and the property
market – the billionaire media owner
overflies border to celebrate the war
dead patriotic as mapping and jamming
airwaves with pastiche to reveal the scumminess
of old ways as the empty template of newness
lets go one iota of consumer claim or
shifting 'need' and 'necessity' out of relative
luxury and tools of self-affirmation. All terms
adapt to the sway of flowers setting fruit,
seeds forming. All that restlessness of triumvirates
and leaders edging towards apotheosis.
Whose speech is eclipsed in the rise
of pharma-gardens, the saviours
in labs. Sentinels testing sentinels.
Nothing times to the almanac
though the almanac was set
in the misalignment to perpetuate
in own images, always imaginal.
Western time surely can't be so blithely
rolled into one, the collapsed sundial
in the failed love garden – cupid upended?

The gardens are isolated relying
on the winds to carry the ingredients
of diversity, as base as both of us
counting the notes bandied about
by birds we insinuate into our wiping
of brow to mark with soil, with dust.
I wonder why you listen to Lou Reed's
'Satellite of Love' when you have no
social contact and remain intact,
deeply involved in vegetable
conversation? And you deplore
the ring-a-ring o' roses band colossus
of starlinks you could follow all the way
to night-gatherings, and fall into barn
owl's eyes happy to let go and be gone.
I am nonplussed. Flowers inimical
set themselves as flowers faulted
Lorenz cypher to make break war
deliverance parent of and yet and yet.

o

Seems we're not at each other's
trenches or reservoirs but calque
of a set of values – no literacy
in horticulture but illumination
in the vascular, in sugars and sun.
Always interlinear reflections,

taking scenes in to set for profit,
somewhere somehow – sustain.
Off notes of decline, 'carbon capture'.
Situational panegyric hoodwink
is still elegiac, nonetheless.
Barely tolerate threshold shepherds
complying with media conference
calls to slash feet on stony ground
where ice illustrated a get-away,
a call to roots and fungicides,
to be left dangling strains
of foot powder. As wry
as la-la land relief – self-
fulfilling Gallus who can only
speak here via a cipher: all these
garden voices accumulated
like a genome, a resequencing
of the chronological you got stuck
within the botanical gardens at another home –
without a dwelling a home that barely
calls you more than a temporary resident. *Repeat.*

I

'Computes its time as well as we'
is what you mean? Little look in.
Industrious as drought, and a paradox
of bees – I love them all, though the blue-banded
bee has been driven out, and flowers adapt.
They will have their zodiacs, and we

our meals, our reward of provision.
Scale and blight windows to other
life is fine to maintain a broader
health, and no slicing to the bone.
No. As if asked to hymn an answer.

o

(((Margin of shade to rise out of tilt and slant of sun)))

Banking would usurp a raised bed avoidance of tetchy
soil, a rocky aftermath of wash-away, of defoliation.
Dwelling settles on the flattened, stake to stake. A gamble.

(((Cloud behind cloud behind cloud and still we burn to cancer)))

Inclusive despoliation cultivates soul of ram – hear call
over valley rise a windmill farm that sunshines deeply,
artesian, and we sit above its collection, sheepless. But we
love the sheep as they surround the van of our brother and his wife
at night and protect to sleep in tune. That's true, and happened,
and cannot be unread in the chewed down garden of paddock –
the field of translation, the bred into industry of roles in the shed.

(((Hear sheep piss together and alone on the stubble not a glint of
green shoots yet)))

Eclipse of weapons is an offset of plough and love and bread
rises fresh as the garden is but a step in rights direction, a dead
without water acknowledgement of the ways of gathering;

to leave a branch sticking over the bed is to arrow the eye,
risk losing sight, but still you let it stay as bird perch,
fount of fertiliser without force, a choice, an absurdist truth.

·I·

Biopsy and biography of the greenhouse and hothouse
specialisms, the fording rivers and directing their flow
with selective naturalism, an art movement in gloves.

When they are gone to elegies, and the stalks and roots
piled high to rot down into a carpet, a spread, what will
displaced words mean, grafts they made overgrow?

And where would they be without their guides and classical
references, so contemplative almost religious without being spiritual,
or is it reverse – planting a seed and a plant outside expectation
    emerging?

o

Negative. These off-centre crops,
these sunblown shades, this heat
in the predicted chill. I utter
valley's brink of evening,
and the herds of dry moss
and curling lichen grow
down from shadecloth above –
the baskets woven out of all extractions,
all processes, cracked – catalyst, 'fluffed',

extruded, set. These overlaps,
this crisis. Farewell. Fare well.

Dream Eclogue

'And to my bedde I gan me for to dresse
Fulfild of thought and besy hevinesse'
CHAUCER, *Parliament of Fowls*

DREAM

Aligned so out of freefall
you make gardens that will
undo in the telling – it's in you
and lacking co-ordinates.
What do you expect
the listener to do with this?
As if their worlds correlate,
as if universal symbols
are perfect translations
of speech and sign and story.

REALITY

Redcap robin spark in grass
as it turns out a misplaced firefear
on a cool day after a cold night
when all is dry reveals senses
in disarray, and that's empirical
to the figurative interior.

DREAM

One disaster lights up another
and with wings you cover the nest
you never made in a first place.
Who accuses prism collapse

to escape from the shaving
machine, the roots waving
upside to catch animations.
Portent is a decision on waking,
which happens again without
escaping, the tendrils of fertilisation,
the injections of pollen, stickiness,
canopy hothouse breath condensing.

REALITY

You watched *La Planète sauvage*
then went straight to bed and fell
into sleep which is rare as normally
you stare at darkness so hard colours
drip from the roof and blur reception.

DREAM

Anticipation as random
planting of ungerminatable
seed-stock piling interminable
retrospectives of blame.

Feathered nests
knocked by a storm
reform and loom
as reactor vessels pressed
against the sunbake freedoms.

REALITY

I can't tell the difference between us:
the daily briefings riding the curve
with an eye to approval as if consensus
is melding with census and as we serve.

DREAM

Verve. Supervivid is the residuum
but no surplus lest its trees which fall
daily behind the scenes you seem.
Seams. Fingers in greening machining all
melting into treatment, and concupiscent
with it; potting-shed elevator heaven scent.

Allegro non troppo dreamt dueting
with Beethoven breathing stars
without voice. Lettuces unable to rise
all year round strangers loved as seedlings.
All in perfect harmony with disruption –
interruptions enter as logical as cultivation.

REALITY

Is not realism, nor vice versa. So near
the surface, always so far from sleep.
All these places I distil over a distance
I can't traverse, can't adequately reconcile –
the eucalypts in the garden at Rosewood Cottage, Schull,

the anomalies of a coastal Irish garden catching
the strains of warmth through the warmth, the ways
of diaspora and the contradictions of growth – roots
not setting so the Atlantic storms upend and toss
down on the old red sandstone rockery, the fuchsias;
or here at 'Jam Tree Gully' as another older tree dies
over a week – leaf by leaf, twig by twig, limb from limb,
the Easter Lilies now dead-headed that gave hope when just a dusting
of rain fell and no other rain followed, or could follow, the ground numb
with evisceration. All these details of the concrete, the installations
of settlement, the crack-up of almanacs and planting programmes.

DREAM

Makes more sense, really – addicted as you are.
Cleaning machine. It's an insult to agency. A far
reach from visionary. You forget the wrens
of there and the wrens of here, the Kerry slug
and the slugs under cans in your garden – spontaneous
generation out of dust to dust, and you wonder
staggering awake what cleared eyed means,
trying to grab it back, narrative. These knowledges
of us on the plate, a transfusion from stem to vein.
And you interpret you immerse – blanche – to explain?

Rusticus Eclogue

"'E's gwâin to leave his farm, as I da larn,"
WILLIAM BARNES

ROBERT

All is aftermath
when you're on the losing end,
and they'll work extra hard to send
him down the harrowed path.

THOMAS

To think they were childhood friends
in an isolated place, and now one sends
the other to the rails, and just to rub it in
offers to buy his old mate out, fuel the sin.

ROBERT

So what was their falling out?

THOMAS

One grew GM canola and contaminated the organic crops of
his mate.

ROBERT

And now the victim will leave his farm?
And few will give a damn?
What of the rest of the shire?
What of the footy team and choir?

THOMAS

The evil bastards Monsanto underwrote
the genetically enhanced substance abuse,
this was never going to be a case they'd lose –
no way they wanted a precedent, to quote
the law speaking to itself, caveat emptor
as a twisted specimen in legal trauma.

ROBERT

To tell the truth, *deep down* I've been wondering which way
to go myself . . . I mean, it's the way of things
now, aint it? The government's pushing
and we've got to keep up with technology.

THOMAS

I am going to refuse their pressure;
trying to make us colonies of America –
make us plant what they want us to plant,
swamp the market so the market grants
benefits to those who comply –
I get sick of being dished out lie
after lie, I get sick of being in the thrall
of a mega corporation that makes us crawl
wealthy shareholders who think they deserve
all the world has to offer up and more – they serve
those who own the seed and are served by them, they store
it up so we come crawling back for more. They claim to feed the poor!

Robert

Well, we're always being told what to do and how
to grow and then there's all this rights stuff,
you know, how we can and can't treat our stock – rough
handling, no mulesing, on and on they go.
And then there's the rubbish about meat
and health – my heart's as strong as an ox's! –
makes my head spin. I mean, some of these do-gooders love the fox
and the numbat – can't have both. A beer? My shout.

Thomas

Not now, mate – I'll take a rain check.
To tell the truth, I'm having a rethink
about how we got about our business.
I mean, the animals having feelings too – their stress
is our stress. And all these poisons we lavish on our paddocks,
they've gotta be affecting our kids. My boy can't concentrate in class.
Enough is enough. We've gotta make science serve us rather
than *us* serve science. I tell ya, I'm for the organic farmer.

Robert

I can't make head nor tail of it. But I do know that he'll be leaving his
    farm
and his erstwhile mate has offered to buy him out. Victory works like
    a charm.

THOMAS

You can wax eloquent when you wanna, Bob, and you've not even
had a drink yet. Actually, I *will* have a beer with you – the crops are
   strong and green!
It's a nasty business, this profit over friendship. Let's keep it in
   perspective.

ROBERT

Too right, my friend. I am sorry he'll lose his farm but we've all
   gotta live.

Eclogue of the 'Big Garden'

for Alan

FARM

The big rigs the big plants the big bins the big yields –
across the stubble-sharp ground the duel duels churlish
but blunt as ambition, no time for hesitation, dragging
the seeder the wishes and predictions, the first rains hope
running out as we seed dry daring rain to come
as from eucalyptus fringes the ringneck parrots' call.
What you hear is the diesel caul and the delivery of smoko.

CITY

The school takes us in with open arms with spread wings
if the fees keeping rolling in rolling like the header across
the grand design the prayer plan for grain accumulation – behave! –
full silos! – for a low 'foreign matter' count at testing time.
As removed as holidays, the thinking back the envisaging
life as it departs from the furrows from the turn of the tractor
the infinity of corners which even the largest blankest paddocks will have

FARM

We could do with the extra hands we could do with the kids
being home but we do this to give them another path out of windrows
and burning-off the big garden that we love and can't see our
way out of the chaff, all contradictions we have foisted in front of us
the spray drum anathemas the conservative politics because
we can't see how else but be conservative, the kids down
in the city hundreds of ks away are going to stray, we know
but warn them against that road taken though we know, we know.

CITY

Rather be reading Judith Wright than fencing
rather be reading Jack Davis than herding
rather find my own way through though a few
extra dollars from hours spent out there is a sunset
in my pocket is the oily residue of ad hoc repairs
is the hessian windbreak over thin bare topsoil
is the glint off the shed when the galahs make an eclipse.
Taste the superphosphate, smell the chook pen,
fret over the fruit trees, tap the water tanks . . .

FARM

Each compulsion to control to eradicate
is legacy is leeway is prestige is kudos
down there with the city kids, we know,
and who is to call them out when we
did it ourselves as young ones – the stamping
out of the mouse plagues, the trophyism
that seems like warning and a forgotten
bill of isolation, a speaking out from space?
They think they grow out of it and we are stuck
on the back of the ute with a spotlight,
but we do it for them, we do *we do*. We see,
we see the wrong and the right of it. We make
the call, and set the alarm earlier and earlier.
They grow away from our ways though we
want the oldest one to come back to us,
to come back and take on the strain,

to say, This is my calling, I am expected.
The voice they expect us to use up here,
but we don't, we are caught in conventions
in the pastoral just as they wish it away.

CITY

I am *not* going back – only to visit
for special occasions, to show off my
lover, my new pact and love that isn't
a farm broken up across title deeds,
with erosions and salinity that are damned
if you do damned if you don't, trenched
to drain the dry when the downpour
comes and makes lowland a quagmire.
I have suggestions – stuff I have learned...
trees to plant, more precision, the place
of community art, a revolution
in the sports centre, so far away.
But no, I will go elsewhere
and *remember*, recall where
I came from, its immensity,
its imprint, its impression
of industry in the big garden
so far from the city, from small towns.
This artifice we are dragged into.

Eclogue of Fire

'Sicelides Musae, paulo maiora canamus!'
VIRGIL, *Eclogue* 4

'A camp fire binds us
Swapping yarns'
CHARMAINE PAPERTALK-GREEN
(writing of her community, the Yamaji people)

SOUL

Out of kilter the fire of wildness,
the kindling of birth we celebrate
such as Villon's 'Épître' to the courtly
child, heavenly conception we announce
the fact in itself of all births, all children,
none elevated above the other and yet
the favours that accrue in government,
the smoke of burning off the wavering
lines in front of a sunny day as aftermath
and what's to come if we don't make epistles
of denial – the birthing rooms of irony,
the bringing to life in a world we burn,
a Golden Age of seventh lines to herald
the new leader who will declare yet
another way through and maintain
or super-increase profits. Humanity's
wriggle room under the sun, the misplaces
of history where we keep position
before falling to crimes of silence.
Learn from the oldest voices
of place passed down – the interfaces
of knowledge burnt is the hellraising
roused by the zeal of words, a word.

Our relationship to the Golden Age
which is the age of fire and suffocation
needs to be reconfigured, an undoing
of the grammar of proximity,
and the figurative realigned
so the sap can course through bodies.
Respect, not copyright. Fire, not conflagration.

SELF

When I was nine I watched fire burning
through 'relieving rain', which vaporised
as it does now shown on the radar before
it even hits the ground. And then older
relatives were gone – out fighting with truck
and water tank and pump and shovel
and wet hessian sack. Through the crops
with anger, and don't think for a moment
the fire fighters almost destroyed didn't
anthropomorphise, because they did.
Most didn't give a damn about the niceties
of rhetoric and device and its broader
implications in the world. World was burning,
which didn't make one fire-fighter's politics
any better than another's however affirming
or negating they might be in ordinary
conversation. In the extraordinary,
the puzzle shifts and positions collapse
into each other. Skin and hair and even bones

burn fast, and a loss is a loss as the caught
animals burn, nesting hollows burst and relapse
into the idea of a future generation. Since
then, I have seen many out of control fires –
bush fires. At twelve I hid under a blanket
in the back of a station wagon as fire burnt
either side of a country road. I have sat
here, inside – not in the garden I try
to make lush in the dry with cooler
nights now, I try to make green against
the colours of burning – I have sat as I now stand,
watching flames and smoke across the valley,
working out how long it will take to reach us,
unless the wind shifts, unless the wind
shifts fire back on itself. And there are great
charred rings of older fires here – of two
and three decades ago, when someone's carelessness
sparked a hill fire that ran and ran,
till it made another layer of record here, too –
a record over the immense traces
these house foundations
can't suppress. Fire in the loop,
which is where we live. Inside a fire storm.

SOUL

You will wake to a sun image with wavy lines
through it – smoke warning. In the 'off-season' –
though there's no such thing now – the time
of 'controlled burns' . . . preparation as thrown

into wartalk, the only way they know. The attack
on supply-lines on undergrowth on 'fuel load':
burning-off to save yourselves from the summers
of your making, these endless summers
of lovelessness. And on the smoke
will ride all the glittering gifts of *nature* –
the first word to deal with in any language –
those miniscule ab-reactions you might
call 'opportunistic'. But you've tapped
every other reservoir for 'resources', so
surely you're not surprised. No, I know
you're not. And they will ask you
the purpose of your research, what 'value
it has to the nation'. None. But to humanity?
You hope, you really hope, and your skin
burns with the shame of having to say so.

SELF

And I have seen the gorse burn out of control
across West Cork despite so many requests
even demands not to burn; and I've seen peat
fires smouldering over years that heat the core
of legitimacy to a record of allusions and museums.
And I have seen forest fires in central Ohio, and watch-
towers that shape themselves to inevitability,
and whole forests ghosts of consequence.
And I have seen pleasure boats burning
on the horizon and it hasn't been a romantic
interlude in speculative fiction loaded with warnings

we can't learn from because it is still entertainment.
And I have seen industrial fires and the eternal
flames of war, and I have seen and heard and smelt
and tasted and dreamt and relived the fires
that ate an entire town and district I lived in.
Fire is beyond the senses. It reaches us before
it is lit, before we perceive it, take it into sensibility.
And yet, fire is the writer of the body's obituary.

SOUL

When you saw the forest burning and the marri trees
exploding with the heat and a tiger snake feeling
towards you, you welcomed it with open arms
but it swept past you, anger in its eyes at your
belief that danger made you want and ceded
worlds within worlds to make them one.
It's not the fire, per se, but its prevalence
its new absolutism, the boost of market
economics, of factory emissions, of your
rapid transport. I separate myself from you
and not even fire can anneal us – some things
will be burnt beyond recognition if you don't
pull back, the very laws that govern the spiritual
upset by your laws of rapacity, your jurisdictions
of greed. And now you sprinkle last year's
fire ash across the garden, hoping it will
decode the trace, open a path to greening.

SELF

We will stop the burning of what doesn't
need to be burnt to survive. We will enhance
the broader conversations over the nature of fire.
We will listen to each of us who knows ways
of fire that nation-states have forced into forgetting.
We will know fire as propellant as literary device
of victory is false grammar. You will show
us how to love the air, to know the balance
of ash and dirt, of living tissue and sky.
We will merge abstraction with realism
and you shall not be forced into conflict.
Your golden age will be contained by us.
Vigour and sparkle and dynamism
will be a taxonomy of growth,
and fire a conceit for itself
or backdrop for billionaire-messianics.

SOUL

There are some fires we are not part of –
shouldn't be and can't be.
Fire contained in itself.
Fire as it speaks with people
who understand and respect it.
Fire that argues with those
who rouse it. Fire makes
and takes stories.
Fire *gardens*.

Eclogue of the Caterpillars in Prime Time

Woolly bear caterpillars
of the tiger moth are
entirely confused by their
naming but some

out in their gardens
are intense out of season
consuming sunflower leaves
and the remodelling

of 'winter', or tracing
the more or less familiar
potatoes and wild oats
to play the seasons'

antiplay of vitality,
of fatalism, the rain
and vegetation issue
the gorging and shitting

and cascading
towards pupating
in the hand so gentle
those thin spins and spirals

coiling into palm (and shitting)
to be let go where it will make a go
of forming its own bureau
of meteorology

on its own but synced
with other waiting pupates
nearby but that's to come
as is the tiger moth

which spent itself laying
some months ago and I adjust
the garden for future
to suit all the collapses,

giving it time and space, too –
a sharing agreement,
a thesaurus of 'invasive'
and 'contradiction',

leaving me the gardener
who sabotages my own crops,
but still finds enough to harvest
more than the leaves of my childhood

with their abjections and wonder,
and that *waiting to see* what they
might become, where I would garden
without damaging – companion to it all.

The Terrifying Prospect of Another Birdless Day, Indoors, Schull, West Cork

The wind driving hard kept the doors and windows closed
and no jackdaws called down the chimney. That was
    yesterday,
a festive day which brought happiness against the flow.

But windows yielded no insights into bird behaviour
against the inclemency of outdoors, where I would flap
around most days, looking into crevices and behind leaves,

but disturbing as little as possible. Seeing without
    consequences,
a kind of wish fulfilment which terrifies because I know
it won't stand up to scrutiny – my own, a wintering

insect's, a wren staying silent and hidden, a stonechat
camouflaging and processing a vocabulary of avoidance.
New words are being added each silence, I am positive.

And today promises more of the same – the terrifying
prospect of another birdless day, a fact I can't unpick –
not having enough zeal to transcend my own limits

of observation, my own thin-on-the ground methodologies
when wind blasts, gales hide Fastnet rock, its lantern,
    under plumes of spray.

Three Arguments with the Elements

1. TELEOLOGICAL ARGUMENT

To go back inside to J. S. Bach's *Brandenburg Concertos*
is no verification – and the red-capped robin
shucking the mist to get the day going
doesn't accord either. That's just an opinion,
isn't it, but I am disordered in my demi-meticulous
approach to the 'outdoor chores' after a few days'
heavy rain. Erosion is a design flaw so easily
'reconfigured'. War does more than *interrupt* – the ground
shook violently some days ago when either the Bindoon
firing range was in active mode or some shot-firer
was dispersing euphemisms. It's not hard to work out
that intelligence tests are tools of conquest –
the red-capped robin was patient enough with my displays
of ignorance staring at the precise points where valley
meets sky, running my eyes along the seam till interrupted
by vegetation, buildings, protruding rocks, and *just* patient
enough to say, Sight isn't a single sense and instinct
is not a control variable, I'm fine-tuning mine as we speak.

2. COSMOLOGICAL ARGUMENT

Nothing comes from everything, said the red-capped robin.
I am not a 'set of genes' and I am not copyright. I am no one's
cause, but I am hoping to mate later today, so don't hang
around.
        I won't! I replied.
                Usually, red-capped robins flit

away quickly, grazing air and twig, but this misty bird
kept me company without giving me priority.

My life is worth no less than yours, it said, and I agreed.
I'm only hanging around because this is the area
that I'm committed to working. This is my zone
and I'm of it. I don't have to explain myself, it insisted,
and even if you give sufficient reason, it won't shift my view.

I opened the red shed and the red-capped robin
didn't follow me in, but hung around the vicinity,
singing a song I wasn't used to, that maybe no other
red-capped robin has sung before. Maybe because
of the mist, but what would I know? I couldn't go
back inside as long as the red-capped robin persisted
in keeping me company. I had no contingency plan
which is distressing, uncanny and, frankly, unusual.

3. ONTOLOGICAL ARGUMENT

Imagine, said the memory of the mist, I will disperse
as the day warms, though so much moisture will be left
on the surface and in the subsoil – day isn't long enough
nor sun concentrated enough to remove my essence.

I am memory and not. When it's drought and you're covered
in dust, you will think of me as a red-capped robin ignites
mid-air. Don' be arrogant – it's *foretold* not foretelling.

All these 'ideas' of contradictory *presence*, all these
anxieties of day-to-day activities, hoping for an imperfect
answer: a silo full of organic grain; fences that hold
out the 'ferals' but allow the wildlife to move through, over.

To go back inside to J. S. Bach's *Brandenburg Concertos* is an argument.
You'll *suddenly* fall through soft ground – a demi-surface –
into an abandoned rabbit warren. It's the closest
you'll have come to a flashback in ages – the mendacity
of chemicals north and south of the valley, the crops urged on,
and remembering a red-capped robin outside broadacre blanks
and residues, that flush of gene-manipulated flowering.

Garden Rondel

Seven silvereyes
and a singing honeyeater
explain to me the manners
of hoeing between rows of brassicas.

They say that hell or high
water is a dry garden's antimony for
seven silvereyes
and a singing honeyeater.

I ward off insect leaf-lovers or leaf-foes
with a shower of garlic-cayenne pepper
concoction – not to hurt, but to deter
just enough, to thwart a fiasco
witnessed by seven silvereyes
and a singing honeyeater.

Coda – Psalms of Sleep: A Psalmistry

as interpreted and versioned by John Kinsella

PSALM 4. TO THE LEAD MUSICIAN OF NEGINOTH. SELAH.

Hear me plead righteousness, God;
as I increase I grow out of distress via you,
hear me singing this prayer.

All twists from truth when we lose good
to shame, and I can but ask all that is endless
against pursuit of vanity and profit, quietly doing our own thing? Selah.

And knowing the Lord has set aside a place aside
for those who are godly brings me hope of recanting this unowned space.
To hear the silence singing.

Out of my sleeplessness, I yearn for the world unfolding
without intervention of greed, and converse with this hope,
curled into a question without doubt as my distress rests in you. Selah.

To claim no special treatment in your less impacting ways
which are not less than many others – trust in grace to lighten the tread.

And when despair overtakes and the desire for more and more
sweeps in to offset a perception of lack, fill the lost's faces
with the warmth of your face that won't burn.

For all the temporary abundance of a reconfigured planet
the bright produce on trestles fades before your bounty.

And shedding anxiety and flames that light the darkness
of the room I close myself into searching for emptiness, I will
let go and embrace sleep in safety of renewal and hope, O Lord.

PSALM 13. TO THE LEAD MUSICIAN.

Will all time pass before you remember me, before you reveal
your face again, O Lord?

How long will the loss of the world around me fill my soul
make a forest of thoughts where there is no forest outside me?
How many days will pass while enemies of life offer life on a plate?

I need you to reach into the emptiness I feel with disaster
with collapse I need you to fill it with light that grows outside,
I need to be free of the death-in-life sleep.

Otherwise, the exploiters will say they bought my vote,
the profiteers will say I have validated their product.

But I know the wrongs of wealth and property will be seen
on the verge of calamity and I will rejoice with others in your generosity.

I will sing long and loud silently and outwardly
because there is still air to breathe and water to drink, O Lord.

PSALM 121. A SONG OF STEPS

When the valley is under stress from gun and chainsaw
I look to the hilltops for a resetting of sunset.

Help comes to this location from all locations all over,
flowing in from the heavens over the earth.

But your foothold will never slip into the wastes
of the rapacious for matter is yours and never sleeps.

God of all the world of all peoples never slumbers
or sleeps and the message of a shared fate echoes.

There is sanctuary in the shade from the side
of house tree rock hills down through the valley.

And there's time to slow and stop the burden of destruction
we have imposed on the sun and the moon – to live.

For the evil comes in so easily so readily via the consuming
of illustrations to decorate our living – our souls aren't in those objects.

Step up to praise the sun but don't mimic it, step down
to let others climb the same steps without manufacturing more –
    O Lord, forever.

PSALM 127. A SONG OF STEPS

The house won't stand without foundations of trust
and the town won't work if people guard only their own.

The insomnia that wracks your life is a strange greed of wakefulness
so difficult to shake in the lateness where body eats dark & light alike.

And children are the gift that is the tree of life, O Lord,
growing through wakefulness and sleep alike.

In laying down their weapons the once powerful become more *powerful*
in claiming no more than the rights of their own consciences, in not
    owning their offspring.

For the children are peacefully and strongly marching against the
    violence
and rapacity of those who rule over them, and they ask for a chance to
    be heard.

Not a God Only Ant Ode – In and Out of the Garden

Ants push god aside emerging from their many tunnels
in what we term a 'colony' while they don't – taking umbrage,
though having the grace to keep to their purpose, concomitant
with god emergent manifold and compelled across interlinked
tunnels with those mouths out of a constellation of gravel.

Over the hill, many different ant IDs cross lines of forage
and traces of godly pheromones paint the pictures many of us
externals don't see with our constrained sense of art. But we
pause to see the meat-ant carrying a moth carcass
eight times its weight and more again if comparing dimensions.

The smallest ants, with their long trails and separated
nests still keeping in contact, are not overwhelmed or squeezed
letting gods in or out, and communicate with more than antennae –
their whole being going into constant exchange. Rubbing. They are not
a machine, or parts of a machine, and are shamed by our definitions.

Odes breaking out of bare ground where ants are most intense sending
their spokes out, cutting through and wearing down through mass
repetition, are not god speaking through ants, but god speaking
as gods with ants, gathering information for use outside the pressing
matter of the collective. God doesn't favour the queen. All ants are godly.

Deterring ants from extending into our comfort zone, our dwelling,
is not a prayer-act, yet has characteristics of prayer as give and take. No
harm done, we want back our sense of having done the right thing,
the selfishness of worship. Blue butterfly passing over green-headed ant,
wasp hovering over bull ant – these are odes, but not the only odes.

Acknowledgements

Agenda, Antipodes, Cincinnati Review, Five Points, Fortnightly Review, Granta, Griffith Review, Michigan Quarterly Review, Paris Review, Prairie Schooner, 'Hymn of the Garden' was commissioned as part of composer Andrew Ford's *Red Dirt Hymns, The Saturday Paper, Out of Time: Poetry from the Climate Emergency* (Valley Press, edited by Kate Simpson).

I wish to acknowledge the Ballardong Noongar people, who are the traditional owners and custodians of the land many of these poems were written on.